the little book of
CONFIDENCE

Edited by
Tiddy Rowan

Hardie Grant

QUADRILLE

The building blocks of confidence
are self-esteem, knowledge, courage,
diligence, compassion, self-discipline,
non-verbal communication skills,
humility and a sense of humour.

"If one advances confidently in the direction of his dreams, and endeavors to live the life which he has imagined, he will meet with a success unexpected in common hours."

HENRY DAVID THOREAU
Walden

Never undervalue yourself.
Remember that you deserve
to have the best life possible.

Set yourself targets.

List down the ten goals you
want to achieve in the next year.

Every task we complete, every obstacle we overcome and every goal we reach gives us a sense of self-accomplishment and self-reliance.

"Let your body tell you you're powerful and deserving, and you become more present, enthusiastic and authentically yourself."

AMY CUDDY
TED Talks

Power posing.

Recent research suggests that if you strike a strong pose — where you take up as much space as possible — your testosterone (dominance hormone) levels increase, whilst your cortisol (stress hormone) levels decrease. Adopting a bigger posture two minutes before a meeting will actually give you more confidence and help you perform better.

Power poses of victory and pride at winning a race or a match are usually expressed by raising the arms in a V and lifting the chin. Power posing is also displayed in the animal kingdom by stretching and expanding postures. It seems to be an instinctive reaction.

The power of body language.

- Placing your hand on your face or your neck is a low-power pose that communicates a need for protection from other people.

- Hiding your hands in your pockets is another example of a low-power pose. Leave your hands free to be expressive.

- Shift your pose to make yourself bigger by easing your shoulders back and opening your torso. This can make you appear more assertive.

- Cultivate a natural smile. The 'Duchenne' smile conveys warmth by a natural contraction of the muscles around the eyes.

"*When I was a child my mother said to me, 'If you become a soldier, you'll be a general. If you become a monk, you'll be the pope.' Instead I became a painter and wound up as Picasso.*"

PABLO PICASSO

Visualise being in a meeting,
gathering or in a presentation.
Empower yourself with a vision
of yourself being assertive, relaxed
and confident.

"No one can make you feel inferior without your consent."

ELEANOR ROOSEVELT
This is My Story

It is easy to get knocked back by other people's negative observations or criticisms. However, it is important to view our vulnerabilities as a strength, not a weakness. We need to find the strength within ourselves to explore and accept others' criticisms without allowing them to damage our self-confidence.

"We either make ourselves miserable, or we make ourselves strong. The amount of work is the same."

CARLOS CASTANEDA
Journey to Ixtlan

Adopting a positive outlook is an important step in developing a confident manner.

"The greater danger for most of us lies not in setting our aim too high and falling short; but in setting our aim too low, and achieving our mark."

MICHELANGELO

Take little steps at first.

Subtle shifts in the way you dress, your body language or even the way you speak are small yet assertive steps towards gaining more confidence.

"*Because of the self-confidence with which he had spoken, no one could tell whether what he said was very clever or very stupid.*"

LEO TOLSTOY
War and Peace

No one else knows what we are really thinking or feeling.

It's easy to forget and important to remember this when you feel as though your lack of confidence is evident to others.

"Fear defeats more people than any other one thing in the world."

RALPH WALDO EMERSON

Sitting around brooding alone at home breeds self-doubt and fear. Sometimes, all that is needed to get rid of anxiety is simply to get out of the house and go for a walk. By removing yourself from your comfort zone, you are starting to combat your fears, which builds your confidence. Although it takes courage, every step will become easier.

"To sing a wrong note is insignificant, but to sing without passion is unforgivable."

LUDWIG VAN BEETHOVEN

"Health is the greatest possession. Contentment is the greatest treasure. Confidence is the greatest friend."

LAO TZU

Keeping fit and physically healthy is essential in maintaining and nurturing your self-esteem. It doesn't have to be excessive – a daily fast walk for half an hour provides a basic formula for discipline and fitness.

"All should be encouraged to reveal themselves, their perceptions and emotions, and to build confidence in the creative spirit."

ANSEL ADAMS

Avoid negative people.

Mantain friendships with people who have positive outlooks and who bring out the best and most confident version of you.

Having informed opinions increases our confidence when communicating with other people. List some of the topics that merit your consideration and develop your own opinions.

> *"Ask with confidence,*
> *listen with humility."*

CHARLIE VAN HECKE
The Art of the Q: Build Your
Business with Questions

"Self-confidence is the first requisite to great undertakings."

SAMUEL JOHNSON

"*This new resolve gave her a sort of light-headed self-confidence: when she left the dinner-table she felt so easy and careless that she was surprised to see that the glass of champagne beside her plate was untouched. She felt as if all its sparkles were whirling through her.*"

EDITH WHARTON
The Mother's Recompense

One of the values that mindfulness teaches us is that thoughts are not facts – they are notions, assumptions and opinions.

So when faced with the thoughts 'I'm out of my depth, I'm afraid, I can't face this', counter it with 'I can manage, I'm not afraid and I can face this'.

"*Do not allow negative thoughts to enter your mind for they are the weeds that strangle confidence.*"

BRUCE LEE
In interview with Joe Hyams

"What I find powerful is a person with the confidence to be her own self."

OPRAH WINFREY

"The image that concerns most people is the reflection they see in other people's minds."

EDWARD DE BONO

Rather than throwing away
a compliment – accept it with
thanks and appreciation.
Remember, it is an expression
of value from the person giving
it to you. People with low self-esteem
tend to turn a compliment
into a negative comment.

There is nothing wrong with suppressing your lack of confidence when in public. Pretending to be more confident and at ease than you actually feel is a key skill. The 'fake it till you make it' mentality actually does boost your confidence in your abilities and will make you feel more assertive in stressful situations.

> *"You can't insure against the future, except by really believing in the best bit of you, and in the power beyond it."*

D. H. LAWRENCE
Lady Chatterley's Lover

"Man often becomes what he believes himself to be. If I keep on saying to myself that I cannot do a certain thing, it is possible that I may end by really becoming incapable of doing it. On the contrary, if I have the belief that I can do it, I shall surely acquire the capacity to do it even if I may not have it at the beginning."

MAHATMA GANDHI

" I know who I am, I know what I can and can't do. I know what I will and won't do."

DOLLY PARTON

The more you focus on getting results, the less your thoughts are consumed by how you're feeling. People with little confidence tend to dwell on how they're feeling, whereas confident people focus their attention on action and have less time to be self-conscious.

Confidence exercise.

- Raise your head up.
- Straighten your back.
- Gently push your shoulders back.
- Take up more space with your pose.

*"Above all, be the heroine
of your life, not the victim."*

NORA EPHRON

"Courage is what it takes to stand up and speak; courage is also what it takes to sit down and listen."

WINSTON CHURCHILL

*"Express yourself completely,
then keep quiet.
Be like the forces of nature:
When it blows, there is only wind;
When it rains, there is only rain;
When the clouds pass, the sun
shines through."*

LAO TZU
Tao Te Ching

Don't lose your balance by constantly struggling through life's events as and when they unfold. Instead, take control and make decisions about what you want out of life and the direction you want your life to take. This proactive approach will enable you to work your way towards achieving the things you want and need.

"We learn little from victory, much from defeat."

JAPANESE PROVERB

Get into the habit of rising to meet challenges rather than shying away from them. The stimulus of really going for it – and more often than not succeeding – empowers you and builds your self-worth.

*"The biggest human temptation
is to settle for too little."*

ANONYMOUS

"To love oneself is the beginning of a lifelong romance."

OSCAR WILDE

Imitate confidence so that when it produces success, it will generate real confidence and self-belief.

**A chance remark can
be uplifting or hurtful.**

In receiving either type of these
remarks let it be a reminder of how we
can contribute to other people's self-
confidence – and, similarly, how we
should take care to avoid damaging it.

"Kindness in words creates confidence. Kindness in thinking creates profoundness. Kindness in giving creates love."

LAO TZU

"*As is our confidence,
so is our capacity.*"

WILLIAM HAZLITT
*Characteristics: In the Manner
of Rochefoucault's Maxims*

Our confidence is also derived from the results of our endeavors; a positive outcome proves to us that we are capable of doing exactly what we set out to do. In turn, this encourages us to go further and have more faith in the extent of our abilities.

Confidence is demonstrated through physical expression. Our nonverbal communication not only governs how others think of us but also how we feel about ourselves. Striking a positive pose conveys to other people our self-confidence, positive demeanor and trustworthiness.

To win, all you need to do is get up one more time than you fall down.

Facing disappointments.

Don't let disappointments get in your way. It is important not to dwell too much when things go wrong. Learn from your disappointments, let them go and move on.

Spend some time – however long
it takes – to figure out what is
meaningful in your life, what you want
to achieve in the future and how you
are going to set out achieving it.

"Confidence is that feeling by which the mind embarks on great and honourable courses with a sure hope and trust in itself."

MARCUS TULLIUS CICERO

Being well-informed on current affairs and general news broadens our perspectives and our conversational breadth. Check headlines, business news, political commentators, sports and entertainment reviews on a regular basis.

"Confidence contributes more to conversation than wit."

FRANÇOIS DE LA ROCHEFOUCAULD

"I am not afraid of storms, for I am learning how to sail my ship."

LOUISA MAY ALCOTT
Little Women

"Our doubts are traitors, and make us lose the good we oft might win, by fearing to attempt."

WILLIAM SHAKESPEARE
Measure for Measure

Be spontaneous and
trust your instincts.

> *"If you hear a voice within you say 'You are not a painter,' then by all means paint, and that voice will be silenced."*

VINCENT VAN GOGH
Letters to Theo van Gogh, 28 October 1883

Our level of confidence is set, to a degree, by how we deal with dissonance in our lives. The difference we feel between what is, what might have been and what might be; the gap between our belief system and its own credibility; between fantasy and reality and the gap we perceive between ourselves and other people. The more we close these gaps the more at ease we feel.

"It is folly for a man to pray to the gods for that which he has the power to obtain by himself."

EPICURUS

"It is not the mountain we conquer but ourselves."

EDMUND HILLARY

Imagine the confidence needed to be a tightrope walker or to abseil up the side of a mountain. Doesn't that make walking into a roomful of people or talking to people at a presentation or party an easy proposition?

"As soon as you trust yourself,
you will know how to live."

JOHANN WOLFGANG VON GOETHE

Find your centre.

Start by thinking where your centre is physically – some people instinctively point to their hearts, others point to the spot between their eyes or to the crown of their head. Once you have established it, have it as a place to return to, a safe centre to your universe when you feel anxious or fearful.

"If we were not all so interested in ourselves, life would be so uninteresting that none of us would be able to endure it."

ARTHUR SCHOPENHAUER

"If you doubt yourself, then indeed you stand on shaky ground."

HENRIK IBSEN

When faced with a situation that heightens your insecurity, practise this exercise.

- Stand firmly on the floor.

- Keep your feet grounded on the floor and the rest of your body will follow suit.

- Focus on your toes and clenching and then releasing them.

- Then allow your shoulders to drop and push them back. Pull an imaginary string up from the top of your head – this lengthens your neck and pulls your head and your chin up.

- Focus your eyes – straight ahead or at 45 degrees – but not downcast on the ground.

It isn't just about being confident, it's about having a belief in other people. If others place their confidence in us, we have a responsibility to justify that belief. Trust is invaluable between friends and in all our human relationships.

"When there is no enemy within, the enemies outside cannot hurt you."

AFRICAN PROVERB

Not only is physical posture important, but the way you present yourself is key to other people's reaction to you.

You may think that everyone around you at a gathering is more socially confident than you, but it is more than likely that many of them aren't – it's just that they are overcoming their inhibitions and fears. Remember, you are not alone in feeling unconfident, but try and rise above your own fear. Concentrate on other people and not your 'self'.

"Life is not easy for any of us. But what of that? We must have perseverance and above all confidence in ourselves."

MARIE CURIE

"Choose a job you love, and you will never have to work a day in your life."

ANONYMOUS

"The only way to be truly satisfied is to do what you believe is great work."

STEVE JOBS

"Confidence is the most important single factor in this game."

JACK NICKLAUS

Self-confidence is an inner belief that you are a powerful, capable and unique human being. This type of confidence exists when you truly know yourself and are aware of your needs, values and abilities.

*"Open yourself to the Tao,
then trust your natural responses:
and everything will fall into place."*

LAO TZU
Tao Te Ching

"*I don't know what your destiny will be, but one thing I know: the only ones among you who will be really happy are those who have sought and found how to serve.*"

ALBERT SCHWEITZER

"I am still determined to be cheerful and to be happy, in whatever situation I may be; for I have also learnt, from experience, that the greater part of our happiness or misery depends upon our dispositions, and not upon our circumstances."

MARTHA WASHINGTON
Letters to Mercy Warren, 1789

"There is only one way to avoid criticism: do nothing, say nothing and be nothing."

ELBERT HUBBARD

"To be yourself in a world that is constantly trying to make you something else is the greatest accomplishment."

RALPH WALDO EMERSON

Motivation exercise.

Choose a motivational picture or quote that empowers you. Make it your laptop screensaver, have it as your home screen on your phone or even place it near your front door so that you can feel inspired by it whenever you need it the most.

You can do it.
You can do it.
You can do it.

"If you have no confidence in self, you are twice defeated in the race of life. With confidence, you have won even before you have started."

MARCUS TULLIUS CICERO

We all have a USP (unique selling point).

Work out what yours is. Feel proud of it, cultivate it and return to it when you need to boost your confidence.

"*I used to walk into a room full of people and wonder if they would like me. Now I look around and wonder if I'm going to like them.*"

ANONYMOUS

It is surprising the time and energy we expend on worrying what other people think of us: our appearance, our intellect and our faults. We should endeavor to break the habit and instead use the time to consider our strengths, our abilities and our best points.

Value yourself highly.

The value you place on yourself is the value that others perceive in you.

Body confidence exercise.

Whenever you start to feel negative
or self-conscious of the way you look,
repeat this mantra 'I am grateful,
proud and above all confident of
my body.'

*"To lose confidence in one's body
is to lose confidence in oneself."*

SIMONE DE BEAUVOIR

Verbal exercise.

Pay attention to how you express yourself. Record yourself during telephone calls and see how you sound when you play yourself back. Do you interrupt? Do you put yourself down? Do you raise your voice at the end of your sentences? Do you seek approval? Do you ask too many questions?

All of these traits are often ascribed to less confident people, so try and address how you can hold a conversation more evenly, ensuring you leave every conversation with the knowledge that you have left a good impression.

"All you need in this life is ignorance and confidence, and then success is sure."

MARK TWAIN
Letters to Cordelia Welsh Foote, 2 December 1887

Emotional security is another confidence building block. Try to keep all of your relationships in good shape.

Don't be afraid to reveal your strengths and qualities to other people. By doing so, you reinforce your own belief system as a potent and effective human being.

*"Beauty begins the moment
you decide to be yourself."*

COCO CHANEL

Don't pin too much hope on future successes, to the point where feelings of anxiety or insecurity occur after a failure. Accept, though, that it is part of the human condition to experience uncertainty, failure and fear at some point.

However, practising mindfulness helps maintain a balanced outlook. It re-focuses our anxious minds to the present moment rather than overly worrying about past or future problems.

Learn to recognise the difference between a constructive criticism and a negative one.

One of the practices of mindfulness is to be non-judgemental. Refraining from expressing judgements frees up your mind to be more understanding and compassionate towards others and yourself.

"So many people are shut up tight inside themselves like boxes... unfolding quite wonderfully, if only you were interested in them."

SYLVIA PLATH
Johnny Panic and the Bible of Dreams

Social psychologist Amy Cuddy has done research into what we are most attuned to when we first meet people. She's discovered we mostly evaluate two key qualities: trustworthiness and confidence.

Be trustworthy and allow people to find confidence in you.

Instant relaxation exercise.

Being confident is synonymous with being relaxed within oneself. Overwrought, over-anxious and overly stressed people rarely exude confidence.

Be aware of your shoulders, drop them and you will automatically feel less tense. Get into the habit of shoulder dropping regularly throughout the day.

"Public opinion is a weak tyrant compared with our own private opinion."

HENRY DAVID THOREAU
Walden and Other Writings

A firm handshake, strong eye contact and a warm smile go a long way to introducing yourself as a confident and self-assured person.

It's important to maintain some level of eye contact during conversation. If, or when, you find that difficult, look at the spot between the other person's eyes.

Being indecisive – especially at work – sends out the signal that you are not sure of yourself or your opinions. Remember that making a decision is better than not making one. And you can always make another one.

*"What matters most is how
well you walk through the fire."*

CHARLES BUKOWSKI

Yes, a glass of wine can give us Dutch courage...

...But it's time to face our fears using the natural inner resources we have inherently developed over the years when faced with life's many obstacles. Rely on these resources and trust them. Seek confidence from within not from outside.

" The greatest way to live with honor in this world is to be what we pretend to be."

SOCRATES

No matter how confident you are
there will always be people whom
you want to impress. Being polite and
having your own opinion, trusting
your own judgment and contributing
original suggestions will make a better
impression than constantly agreeing
and towing the party line.

"*It is the mark of an educated mind to be able to entertain a thought without accepting it.*"

ARISTOTLE

Even when you don't feel like it –
especially when you don't feel like it
– practise maintaining a cheerful and
enthusiastic outlook.

All animals have confidence as part of their natural birthright.

In essence, we need to return to our natural primal, confident state and forget our human concerns and our social preoccupations.

Beyond nature – nurture also plays a role in the developing child's confidence. Behavioural geneticists Corina Greven of King's College in London and her colleague Robert Plomin of the Institute of Psychiatry conducted research published in June 2009 on the heritability of self-confidence and its relationship to IQ and performance. Greven and Plomin found that children with a greater belief in their own abilities often performed better at school, even if they were actually less intelligent.

www.psychologytoday.com

Even inherent confidence still has to be nurtured from a young age.

"What we learn only through the ears makes less impression upon our minds than what is presented to the trustworthy eye."

HORACE

In the first thirty seconds of meeting, people form an opinion of who you are, through your body language, eye contact, expressions, style, levels of confidence and competence.

You never get a second chance
of making a good first impression.

Small talk.

Lots of people find small talk boring or meaningless. But actually it allows people to gauge more about the other person than just their appearance, pitch or credentials. It has even been proven that five minutes of small talk before a business deal increases the amount of value made in the negotiation.

"Success is most often achieved by those who don't know that failure is inevitable."

COCO CHANEL

Remember to like yourself.

You're the one you're going home with, so it's important you stay good friends with yourself.

If your personality falls into the quiet category or the more introverted type who is happier staying at home – then it's time to step out. Going out once a week is not a tall order – organise something to do with a friend or a group of friends.

Being in control rather than being controlled is part of maintaining our self-esteem and confidence. Regularly assessing our lives – our goals and how happy we are – allows us to work out what we still want to achieve in life. A daily routine of contemplation or mindfulness will provide the mental space and time to do this.

" The greater the artist, the greater the doubt. Perfect confidence is granted to the less talented as a consolation prize."

ROBERT HUGHES

You can't *buy* confidence. You have to build it yourself. But it's free and attainable.

Breathing techniques.

When you're faced with a roomful of people, a presentation or an important dinner, practise some breathing exercises before you go in.

Three breaths:
'In' for a count of four.
'Hold' for two counts.
'Let out' slowly for five counts.

Let your 'out' breath be longer than your 'in' one and you will feel more at ease.

Tips for confident public speaking.

- Work to control filler words.

- Practice, pause and breathe.

- Greet some of the audience members as they arrive. It's easier to speak to a group of friends than to strangers.

- Know the room. Arrive early, walk around the speaking area and practise using the microphone and any visual aids.

- Relax. Begin by addressing the audience. It buys you time and calms your nerves. Pause, smile and count to three before saying anything. Transform nervous energy into enthusiasm.

- Realize that people want you to succeed. Audiences want you to be interesting, stimulating, informative and entertaining. They're rooting for you.

- Don't apologize for any nervousness or problem – the audience probably never noticed it.

- Concentrate on the message – not the medium. Focus your attention away from your own anxieties and concentrate on your message and your audience.

TOASTMASTERS INTERNATIONAL

www.toastmasters.org

"*The moment you doubt whether you can fly, you cease forever to be able to do it.*"

J.M. BARRIE
Peter Pan

A technique that's commonly used in helping people dispel their negative thoughts is to say the word 'stop' either internally or out loud, when a destructive thought presents itself.

A lot of time can be wasted on thinking about material things we don't have or circumstances that are not in our favour. A positive override here is to think of the things we do have and the circumstances that are favourable.

"I was always looking outside myself for strength and confidence, but it comes from within. It is there all the time."

ANNA FREUD

Memory in conversation.

When introduced to a new individual
or group at a party, social gathering
or at work, ensure that you make a
habit of remembering their names.
The name's the thing. If you can
stretch your memory further, it
is worthwhile remembering one
particular fact about each person.
When you later reiterate the fact back
to them, they immediately feel as
though you are both interested and
trustworthy. In short, you have gained
their confidence.

"Self-confidence depends on environment: one does not speak in the same tone in the drawing room as in the kitchen."

GUSTAVE FLAUBERT
Madame Bovary

Social situations are often challenging to introverts or people who suffer from low self-confidence. However, understanding what might be expected of you in social situations will help you feel better equipped, prepared and less apprehensive. So it is worth spending a little time beforehand working out what you may be required to talk about.

At times when your confidence is at a low ebb, think back to times when you have felt truly confident in life. It's worth recalling those moments and reflecting on them in order to reinforce your self-belief.

"The big gap between the ability of actors is confidence."

KATHLEEN TURNER

Building block of confidence.

Be curious.

Be spontaneous.

Be brave.

Take risks.

Go on adventures.

Forget your inhibitions.

Believe in yourself.

Trust yourself.

Love yourself.

Remember it's now or never.

"Once we believe in ourselves, we can risk curiosity, wonder, spontaneous delight, or any experience that reveals the human spirit."

E.E. CUMMINGS

Seek out a 'confidence buddy'.

Select someone who you trust and whose opinion you respect. Explain you are embarking on a confidence-building programme. They can film videos of you, do voice recordings, monitor your facial expressions whilst you talk, give you feedback on your appearance. They can also go to parties and observe how you interact with others and help you approach and meet new people.

Broaden the colour schemes you wear. If you tend to stick to neutrals, beiges and sombre colours, try adding splashes of colour. It's a technique called 'peacocking' as colour grabs people's attention.

"Men acquire a particular quality by constantly acting a certain way."

ARISTOTLE

"Be who you are and say what you feel, because those who mind don't matter, and those who matter don't mind."

BERNARD M. BARUCH

Be present.

During an interview our nerves can often get in the way of our clarity of thought. Often it becomes hard to focus on what the interviewer is actually asking.

The key to coming across as confident in both your answers and your manner, is to stay present. Focus your mind on what is actually happening. Listen to the questions carefully and give clear, concise answers. A relaxed and present mind will be able to provide the answers you have previously prepared.

"We often refuse to accept an idea merely because the tone of voice in which it has been expressed is unsympathetic to us."

FRIEDRICH NIETZSCHE

So if we want to get our ideas across, we need to work on our delivery as well as the content.

Being happy undoubtedly helps keep us in a confident state of mind.

Make a list of 10 things in life that make you happy and remind yourself of them on a daily basis.

Everything in the material world is transitory. Sensory pleasure derived from material things is more fleeting than the pleasure derived from nature. Focusing more on the non-material rather than the never-ending desire for material things creates a confidence in accessible pleasure, and diminishes relentless cravings.

"Do one thing every day that scares you."

ELEANOR ROOSEVELT

What is the worst thing that could happen when you approach someone at a party or gathering? What is the worst thing that could happen when you are addressing a group of people in a presentation or speech? Don't let fear get in the way. Reframe everything to being within your capability and means.

If you're lucky enough to be in good health – be glad, be grateful and be confident.

As your confidence grows and you achieve more success, return the favour to others. Give credit to people's endeavors, ideas and accomplishments. Pay them compliments and praise them. Remember – they, too, are striving towards their own goals and there will always be more for us to learn.

Celebrate your strengths and successes, but remember the journey you have taken to achieve them.

BIBLIOGRAPHY

Books mentioned in *The Little Book of Confidence*

Alcott, Louise May, *Little Women* (Signet Classics, 2012)

Barrie, J.M, *Peter Pan* (Wordsworth Editions, 1993)

Bukowski, Charles, *What Matters Most is How Well You Walk Through the Fire* (Ecco, 1999)

Castaneda, Carlos, *Journey to Ixtlan* (Washington Square Press, 1991)

Flaubert, Gustave, *Madame Bovary* (Wordsworth Classics, 1993)

Hazlitt, William, *Characteristics: In the Manner of Rochefoucault's Maxims* (Forgotten Books, 2012)

Lawrence, D.H., *Lady Chatterley's Lover* (Penguin Classics, 1995)

Plath, Sylvia, *Johnny Panic and the Bible of Dreams: Short Stories, Prose and Diary Excerpts* (Harper Perennial, 2008)

Roosevelt, Eleanor, *This is My Story* (Harpers & Brothers publications, 1937)

Shakespeare, William, *Measure for Measure* (Oxford paperbacks, 1998)

Thoreau, Henry David, *Walden and Other Writings* (Bantam Press, 1980)

Tolstoy, Leo, *War and Peace* (Penguin Classics, 1982)

Tzu, Lao, *Tao Te Ching* (Hackett Publishing, 1993)

van Hecke, Charlie, *The Art of the Q: Build Your Business with Questions* (CreateSpace Independent Publishing Platform, 2014)

Virgil, *The Aeneid* (Bloomsbury, 2007)

Wharton, Edith, *The Mother's Recompense* (Little, Brown, 1998)

Woolf, Virginia, *An Unwritten Novel* (Swinburne Press, 2013)

Websites

www.psychologytoday.com/blog/wired- success/200907/self-confidence-nature-or-nurture

www.ted.com

www.ted.com/talks/amy_cuddy_your_body_language_shapes_who_you_are

www.toastmasters.org

PAGE REFERENCES

Page 10: www.ted.com/talks/amy_cuddy_your_body_language_shapes_who_you_are

Page 33: Van Hecke, Charlie, *The Art of the Q: Build Your Business with Questions* (CreateSpace Independent Publishing Platform, 2014)

Page 156-157: www.toastmasters.org

Page 158: Barrie, J. M., *Peter Pan* (Wordsworth Editions, 1993)

QUOTES ARE TAKEN FROM:

Albert Schweitzer was a German theologian, philosopher and physician.

Amy Cuddy is a social psychologist specialising in confidence.

Anna Freud was the founder of psychoanalytic child psychology along with Melanie Klein.

Ansel Adams was an American photographer and enviromentalist.

Aristotle is one of greatest philosophers from ancient Greece, his work has had a long-lasting influence on the development of all Western philosophical theories.

Arthur Schopenhauer was a German philosopher best known for his book *The World as Will and Representation* published 1818.

Bernard M. Baruch was an American financier, statesman and philanthropist.

Bruce Lee was a martial artist who went on to become an actor.

Carlos Castaneda was an American author who wrote a series of books on shamanism.

Charles Bukowski was an American writer, poet and author. He wrote over 60 books; *Time* described him as the 'laureate of American lowlife'.

Charlie Van Hecke is the author of *The Art of the Q: Build Your Business with Questions*.

Coco Chanel was a French fashion designer, she called her brand 'Chanel'.

D. H. Lawrence was an author, who most famously wrote the controversial novel *Lady Chatterely's Lover*.

Dolly Parton is a famous American singer-songwriter.

E.E. Cummings was of the most influential and revered of the Modernist poets.

Edith Wharton was an American author who is most well known for her novel *The Age of Innocence*, which centers on the 1870s New York upper-class society.

Edmund Hillary was the first man to reach the summit of Mount Everest alongside Nepalese Sherpa mountaineer Tenzing Norgay.

Edward De Bono is a proponent of lateral thinking and has written a book called *Six Thinking Hats*.

Elbert Hubbard was an American writer and publisher.

Eleanor Roosevelt was an American politician and the longest-serving First Lady of the United States.

Epicurus was an ancient Greek philosopher who founded the school of thought called Epicureanism.

François de La Rochefoucauld was a French noble and author.

Friedrich Nietzsche was a German philosopher in the 19th century who coined the phrase 'God is dead'.

Gustave Flaubert was an influential French writer, most famously known for his first novel *Madame Bovary*.

Henrik Ibsen was a 19th century Norwegian playwright, known as 'the father of realism'.

Horace was the leading Roman lyric writer.

Henry David Thoreau was a writer whose masterpiece was *Walden* (1845).

Jack Nicklaus is a retired American professional golfer.

J.M. Barrie was a Scottish writer, most notably known for his children's masterpiece *Peter Pan*.

Johann Wolfgang von Goethe was a German poet, playwright and novelist and is considered the greatest German literary figure of the modern era.

Kathleen Turner is an American actress.

Lao Tzu was a philosopher of ancient China and author of Tao Te Ching.

Leo Tolstoy was a Russian writer, regarded as the best writer of his age. His two most famous novels are *Anna Karenina* and *War and Peace*.

Louisa May Alcott was an American novelist most famous for her book *Little Woman* published in 1868.

Ludwig van Beethoven was a German pianist and is one of the greatest composers of all time.

Mahatma Gandhi was the leader of the Indian nationalist movement against British rule in India.

Marcus Tullius Cicero is considered one of Rome's greatest orators.

Marie Curie conducted pioneering research on radioactivity.

Mark Twain wrote *The Adventures of Tom Sawyer* and its sequel, *Adventures of Huckleberry Finn*.

Martha Washington was the wife of George Washington, the first president of the United States

Michelangelo was a High Renaissance painter, sculptor, architect and engineer.

Niccolò Machiavelli was a historian during the Renaissance.

Nora Ephron was a screenwriter and playwright.

Oprah Winfrey is an American talk show host.

Oscar Wilde was an Irish writer, playwright and poet. He is best known for his book *The Picture of Dorian Grey* and his play *The Importance of Being Earnest*.

Pablo Picasso was a Spanish painter, regarded by many as the most important artist of the 20th century.

Plato is considered to be one of the most important Greek philosophers.

Robert Hughes was an Australian art critic famed for his vitriol.

Ralph Waldo Emerson was an American preacher, philosopher, lecturer and poet, and the leader of the Transcendentalist movement.

Samuel Johnson was one of the most famous English literary figures of the 18th century.

Simone de Beauvoir was a French writer who significantly influenced both feminist existentialism and feminist theory.

Socrates was a classical Greek philosopher.

Steve Jobs was an American entrepreneur and inventor, who was the co-founder, chairman and CEO of Apple Inc.

Sylvia Plath was an American poet, writer and author and is often described as advancing the genre of confessional poetry. Her most famous novel was entitled *The Bell Jar*.

Theodore Roosevelt was the 26th president of the United States.

Thomas Merton was a Trappist monk and peace and civil rights activist.

Vincent Van Gogh is the most well known Post Impressionist painter, however he was neither successful or financially stable throughout his life.

Virginia Woolf was a member of the Bloomsbury group and the author of *Mrs Dalloway* and *A Room of One's Own*.

William Hazlitt was a writer, art critic and humanist.

William Shakespeare was an English poet, actor and playwright. He is now considered one of the greatest writers in the English language and his works include, *Hamlet*, *Macbeth* and *King Lear*.

Winston Churchill was the British Prime Minister during the war years of 1940-1945 and again in 1951-1955.

Editorial director Anne Furniss
Creative director Helen Lewis
Editor Romilly Morgan
Editorial assistant Harriet Butt
Designer Emily Lapworth
Production director Vincent Smith
Production controller Emily Noto

First published in 2015 by Quadrille, an imprint of Hardie Grant Publishing

Quadrille
52–54 Southwark Street
London SE1 1UN
quadrille.com

Reprinted in 2015, 2016 (four times), 2017 (four times), 2018 (thrice), 2019
20 19 18 17 16 15 14

British Library Cataloguing-in-Publication Data: A catalogue record for this book is
available from the British Library.

ISBN: 978 1 84949 515 8

Printed in China